Presented to:

_____

From:

_____

Date:

_____

THE GREATEST SOLDIER WHO EVER LIVED

Daniel R. Johnson

Providence
PUBLICATIONS

P.O. Box 882 • Kokomo, IN 46903-0882

The truths in this book surrounding the life and ministry of Jesus Christ are factual. All other characters are fictional.

THE GREATEST SOLDIER WHO EVER LIVED

published by Providence Publications

© 1999 by Daniel R. Johnson

Library of Congress Catalog Card Number: 99-64155

International Standard Book Number: 0-9671383-1-0

Book and cover design by James W. Johnson

Printed in the United States of America

Scripture quotations are from the King James Version (KJV).

For information:
PROVIDENCE PUBLICATIONS
P.O. Box 882 • Kokomo, IN 46903-0882

With gratitude to . . .

the thousands of valiant soldiers

who sacrificed their lives

on battlefields around the world,

allowing me to live a life filled

with freedom and opportunity.

I HAVE BEEN GIVEN a lot of gifts in my life—some expensive, some sentimental, and some unwanted. When I first saw this one, it seemed to fall somewhere between sentimental and unwanted. Yet as time would prove, this gift has changed my

life. It is a framed photograph of my grandfather wearing his army uniform. According
to my dad it was taken sometime following
World War II.

It struck me as a sentimental gift because I
received it while at my grandfather's house on
the day of his funeral. He had died after a
long struggle with cancer. Dad was an only
child, and so the only ones there were my
parents, my two sisters and their husbands,
and my wife and I.

Understandably, the day included a lot of

tears and stories from my dad about the "good old days." As we were sharing some childhood memories, my dad brought out several boxes that contained things that our grandfather wanted us to have. At first I questioned whether or not the timing was appropriate to sort through Grandpa's possessions, but since he wanted us to have them, we began to look through them.

One of the boxes had a set of antique dishes for my sister Susan and another one contained an old hand-stitched quilt for my sister Mary. They both remembered times when they had told our grandmother how much they liked them.

Underneath the old quilt was the photograph of my grandfather. It surprised me, because I can't remember ever seeing it before, and I know that I hadn't requested it. My dad remembered my grandmother keeping it on her dresser, but since she had died he hadn't seen it. But here it was, and for some reason my grandfather wanted me to have it.

In all honesty, the picture not only surprised me, it also disappointed me, because I really didn't want it. After all, what was I going to do with an old picture of my grandfather? For all practical purposes, it was worthless. Don't misunderstand. I loved Grandpa, but the two of us were never very close. He was from a different generation, and at times it seemed as if he was from a different world. I never really figured him out.

I remember a time when I was a teenager—I think it was during a political campaign—when I said something in my grandfather's presence that was critical of the military. I thought he was going to take my head off! He said something about this country being the greatest place on earth to live and that if we didn't stand up for freedom, then who would?

From that moment on, I knew that criticizing the country, and especially the military, in front of my grandfather was not a very good idea. It was also about that time that my dad told me that Grandpa had seen a lot of combat in World War II. He didn't talk much about the war, but it had made a huge impact

on his life. With my dad's strong encourage-
ment, I stopped sharing my immature views
with my grandfather. As a matter of fact,
from that time on I don't remember ever hav-
ing a meaningful conversation with him. The
last time I saw him was at my grandmother's
funeral last year. Since then, he invited us to
visit several times, but we never did.

In light of our less-than-warm history, this
picture seemed like a strange gift. So after
making a couple of awkward expressions of
appreciation, I put it into the pile of things

that we needed to take home.

A couple of days later I found the old picture, zipped into a pocket in my suitcase. I guess I had overlooked it when I unpacked. As I was looking at it, trying to decide what to do with it, I noticed that the backing of the frame was bulging. Earlier, I hadn't paid close enough attention to notice it. When I took the backing off to find out what was wrong, I found an envelope with my name on it. The handwriting was my grandfather's. All of a sudden, this gift became rather interesting.

My first emotion was greed. *"Maybe it's some old stock certificates from the '40s that are now worth millions!"* That dream, however, was quickly shattered when I saw that it was a letter written to me from my grandfather. I can't remember ever receiving a letter from him before, but in light of the circumstances, I decided to sit down and read it. Here's what he wrote:

❖   ❖   ❖

Dear Tom,

I hope that you find this letter. I asked

your father to give you this picture, and knowing that you're the curious type, I didn't think it would take you very long to find it. I suppose you were surprised to receive a picture of me, but since you are my only grandson, I wanted you to have it.

I regret the fact that we were never very close to one another. I can remember a few times when you stayed with your grandmother and me when you were young, but I never really got to know you. I always had such a hard time figuring you out. For that matter, I struggled to understand your whole generation.

At the same time, I don't suppose you ever quite figured me out. I probably appeared to you to be an old man who was set in his ways and judgmental of others. For most of my life, that was true. But Tom, in the past few years I've come to recognize the mistakes that I have made, and I've been trying to correct them. One of those mistakes was not getting to know my only grandson.

Even though I've given up on the idea of

establishing any kind of real relationship with you, I want to ask you to forgive me for not being a better grandpa. I also want you to understand a little bit about who I am. As I near the end of my life on earth, I've come to believe that it is very important for you to understand your heritage.

Please realize that I wanted to tell you all of this in person when I saw you at your grandmother's funeral, but you had to leave right away, and so I never got the opportunity. Now, with the way I'm feeling (my doctor claims that the chemotherapy is helping, but I don't believe him), I've decided to write you this letter.

I was born in 1925, while World War I was still a vivid memory. I know that it's hard for many people to understand today, but America was a very different place in those days. Times were tough. The stock market crashed when I was just 4 years old, and so my earliest memories are of The Great Depression.

Because of the economic conditions, my dad (your great-grandfather) lost the little store that he owned in New Jersey. Even though I was young, I can still remember the look of pain in my father's face when he explained to my sisters and me that we would have to move to my grandparents' farm.

We made new friends and were able to go to school, but after school and during the summers, we had to work on the farm. It was a hard life, but we felt fortunate to be around family and to have enough to eat. Even though we were poor, in a strange way we didn't *feel* poor, because in those days virtually everyone was poor.

When your father was growing up, there were times when I was jealous of him. I remember watching him ride his bike and playing with his other toys, wishing that I had been able to enjoy such a carefree childhood. I guess it was because of my childhood experiences that I was so determined to give him the opportunities that I had missed out on.

The United States became involved in World War II while I was in high school. I'll never forget the day when we heard the news about the Japanese attack at Pearl Harbor. I had never heard of Pearl Harbor before. Our family listened to President Roosevelt on the radio (we didn't have TV back then) as he explained what had happened. As you probably know, he called it "a date which will live in infamy," a description that was certainly true.

As we sat in my grandparents' house that night, everyone knew that if the war lasted very long I would probably have to go; but no one was willing to say a word about it. Today, you know that we won the war, but back then we weren't nearly so confident. Looking into the future in December of 1941 was frightening and grim. Fortunately, I was able to graduate from high school in the spring of 1943. As soon as school was out, instead of waiting to be drafted, I joined the Army.

It was hard leaving home. My parents, sisters and even my grandparents all saw me off at the train station. Your grandmother was also at the train station that day. We had known each other through high school and had talked about getting married, but we both knew that the outcome of the war could change everything. Very little was said that day, even though we were all thinking the same thing: *this could be our final goodbye.*

My mother and your grandmother cried the whole time. As I said goodbye to my dad he didn't cry, but I saw that same look on his face that I had seen as a boy when he told us about losing the store. Now he was afraid that he might lose his only son. Looking through the window of the train, watching everyone I loved fade into the distance, was the most difficult experience I had ever gone through. Unfortunately, I had many more difficult experiences ahead of me.

Basic training didn't seem too bad to me. In hindsight, I guess the long days and hard work on the farm had prepared me pretty well for the physical challenges of the training. As soon as it was over, we were sent to England.

We were all afraid, but we knew that our freedom depended upon winning this war. We were willing—and in some ways even eager—to go and get the job done. We dearly loved our country, and we were willing to pay any price for its freedom. Not long after arriving in England, we began to train for the inevitable invasion of the European continent. As we trained, it quickly became clear that we would probably play a central role in the invasion.

The preparation was intense. While in England, we trained in the field for days at a time. In a strange way, most of us wanted to get on to the real thing. For some reason, we didn't think that actual combat could be much worse than the training, but it was! My first combat experience was on June 6, 1944: D-Day.

As we boarded the ship to cross the English Channel, we were handed a letter from General Eisenhower. It was intended to motivate us and cause us to realize that the hopes and dreams of freedom-loving people everywhere were depending upon us. I kept the letter and later had it framed and displayed in my office.

The ride across the Channel was pretty rough, especially when we got into the little Higgins boats that took us to shore. We were all crammed tightly together, we were scared —and I got seasick.

We landed at Omaha Beach in the morning of June 6. I think it was around 7 o'clock. (It still feels like yesterday!) The combination of adrenaline and fear that I felt during those early morning hours still haunts me. Even now, fifty-two years later, I have nightmares about jumping out of the boat and into the water off the Normandy coast.

Since the war I have told almost no one about my battle experiences—partly because the memories are so painful, but also because words can't begin to describe what it was like! I hope and pray that you will never have to go through anything like it. As our boat approached the shore, we came under heavy German fire. When the door opened, we jumped into water that was a lot deeper than we expected. It was all we could do not to drown under the weight of our gear.

For some, drowning may have been the merciful way out. German machine gun fire was relentless. We were like ducks in a shooting gallery. Many of the guys died before they hit the water. I learned later that some boats had casualty rates of 90%. The water between the boats and the shore was red with blood. All I could think of was survival. I lost most of my gear in the water. If I hadn't, I probably would have drowned.

As I made my way toward the shore, I felt a sharp pain in my right leg. I didn't know what it was at first, but I soon realized that I had been shot. That was the first of two times I was wounded during the war. Fortunately, it was only a flesh wound, so I bandaged my leg myself. Later in the day, a doctor would clean and stitch the wound.

Those of us who made it to shore alive were cold, wet, and afraid that our mission was falling apart. I can't begin to explain what it was like on Omaha Beach. Dead bodies were everywhere, gunfire was raging, and many of the wounded were screaming in pain.

Unfortunately, D-Day was only the beginning of my wartime experiences. It's impossible to describe to you what it was like to shoot and kill other human beings, most of whom were just as young and scared as me. It was a horrible feeling, but it didn't take me long to learn that if I didn't kill them, they would kill me. I don't know if it's surprising or not, but I have never fired a weapon since the war.

As I said, I was wounded twice during the war. The second time was just before Christmas in 1944. The Germans had mounted a counterattack during the fall of '44. They had been making a lot of progress, and we were on the defensive.

We had come under pretty heavy fire, and so my buddy Frank and I dove into a ditch to take cover. Before I made it in, I was shot in the shoulder. Frank did the best he could to stop the bleeding and to dress my wound. We ended up spending the night in that ditch.

I honestly thought that I was going to die. We were both so scared and cold that neither of us could sleep, so we spent most of the time telling each other stories about home. I ended up crying a lot that night, wanting so badly to go home. We made it out the next morning and I was taken to an army hospital.

I feel incredibly blessed to have made it out of World War II alive. Many were not nearly so fortunate. During the war, 292,000 Americans were killed, and more than 1.7 million returned home injured in some way. The United States spared nothing in our quest for victory.

Some of the best and bravest men I have ever known died in World War II. To this day, I find myself lying awake at night wondering, *"Why did I get to live, when so many died?"* I wasn't a better soldier, but for reasons known only to God, I made it home alive.

One of the happiest days of my life was the day when the train pulled into my hometown. The mood that day was so different from the mood when I had left. This time the tears were tears of joy, and the look in my father's eyes was a look of pride rather than pain.

I suppose your parents have told you a lot of what happened in the years after the war. Your grandmother and I were married six months after I arrived home. Two years later, your dad was born. In an odd way, as horrible as the war was, the years that followed were wonderful. The GI bill paid my way through college, and then I was able to go on to law school.

In 1954, I founded the law firm that your dad now runs. Even though you like practicing law in the city, I am still hopeful that someday you'll move back home and join your dad at the firm. I am hoping that one of your boys will choose to go into law and carry on the family tradition.

I never could have dreamed of all the opportunities that I have received since the war. Instead of coming home to a withdrawn and depressed country, I came home to a thriving, growing, and exciting one. We bought a car, we bought a house, and life has been filled with an ever-expanding list of privileges and benefits.

Although I don't want to sound proud, I've always believed that the sacrifice of the 12 million Americans who wore the uniform during World War II led to the opportunity that our country has enjoyed ever since.

Tom, I am telling you all of this because I want to pass on to you the most important lesson that I have ever learned. This solitary truth has changed my life: Great love will lead to great sacrifice, and great sacrifice will lead to great opportunity.

In a way, I have lived this lesson throughout my lifetime. My love for my country motivated me to be willing to sacrifice it all on the battlefields of Europe.

After the war, my generation then built the greatest opportunities for peace, prosperity, and happiness in the history of the world. Again, I don't want to sound proud, because I am only one small man in the midst of a huge country, but I think that history clearly teaches that as our generation planted sacrifice, your father's generation harvested opportunity. Thankfully, your dad received and then passed those opportunities on to you.

Even though I have lived this lesson about love, sacrifice, and opportunity for over fifty years, its significance never hit me until just a few years ago when I spent some time with my old friend Frank.

Frank and his wife Emily traveled with your grandmother and me to France for the 50th anniversary of D-Day. Neither of us had been back to Europe since the war, and so, as you can imagine, it was quite an emotional journey. Early one morning, while the women were still asleep in the hotel, Frank and I took a walk together through the U.S. cemetery at Normandy. It is a breathtaking sight. If you ever get a chance, you ought to visit it.

Today, the rows of crosses that mark the graves and the quiet beach below are a far cry from the noise and agonizing activity of my first Normandy visit. After we reminisced awhile about some of our experiences during the war, Frank started talking about love, sacrifice, and opportunity. He did so by telling me the story of a soldier who lived many years ago.

Like those of us who were born during the 1920s, the soldier whom Frank told me about was also born during a time of great difficulty and darkness. Just as we did in World War II, this soldier also went to a faraway land to fight for freedom. He was motivated by the deepest love imaginable, expressed the greatest sacrifice in history, and created the most magnificent opportunity for all mankind. The soldier Frank told me about wasn't just anybody; He was Jesus, the greatest soldier who ever lived.

As we walked along the now quiet cliffs of Normandy, Frank reminded me about how we felt as we landed on that enemy beach. "Just think," he asked, "how Jesus must have felt 2,000 years ago when He landed on enemy Earth?"

Tom, as we walked through the cemetery that morning, I realized for the first time in my life that the story of Jesus is not simply a cute story for children, or a religious fairytale for weaklings. At age sixty-nine, I *finally* recognized that Jesus' story is a soldier's story about love and sacrifice creating opportunity.

I had gone to church a few times with your grandmother, and so I had heard that Jesus was God's only Son, but no preacher had ever explained it the way Frank did that morning in Normandy. He told me that Jesus came to earth not to conquer but to liberate. He also told me that God loves every child, every man, and every woman who lives on the face of the earth. In fact, God loves the world so much that He sent Jesus to earth to rescue people from their prison camp of sin.

Jesus was born into a dangerous world, behind enemy lines. From day one He was "under fire," just as we were when we stepped out of the boats in the early morning hours of D-Day. The first enemy soldier Jesus encountered was a king named Herod who tried to kill Him.

When Jesus was just a toddler, King Herod urged the visiting wisemen from the East to reveal Jesus' location. When they refused, he ordered every male child two years of age and under to be killed. Just think, Tom, your little

Zachary is not yet two. Can you imagine living in a country where every baby boy was to be located, taken into custody, and then murdered? That was the world into which Jesus was born!

I remember seeing the fear and emptiness on the faces of the people who had endured Hitler's rampage of Europe. Other soldiers told me how scared and broken the people were that they rescued from the concentration camps. My guess is that Jesus saw that same kind of pain and brokenness when He looked into the eyes of the people whom He came to rescue.

When Jesus was thirty years old, He publicly and actively began to engage the enemy in battle. Unlike the war in which I fought, Jesus' battles were not fought with bombs, rifles, or bayonets, but with the truth of God, the performance of miracles, and the compassion of godliness.

Tragically, Jesus' enemies were not willing to surrender without a fight. I remember Frank saying, "Jesus was constantly being attacked by a band of religious warriors called Pharisees, but every time they attacked, they did more damage to themselves than to Jesus." Through it all, Jesus never backed down; He never accepted the enemy's values; and He consistently and completely followed His Father's will.

As we walked and talked that morning in Normandy, Frank reminded me how our hatred of the enemy intensified with every passing day of battle. Jesus, however, offered His enemies numerous chances to surrender and join the forces of freedom. Frank pulled a little New Testament out of his pocket and read me Jesus' words in Matthew 11 that say, *"Come unto Me, all ye who labor and are heavyladen, and I will give you rest."*

Only a few accepted His liberating offer. Jesus put together a squad of twelve men. Yes, there were others who supported His cause from behind the lines, but for the most part the only ones who fought alongside Jesus were those twelve. Even then, one of them would later betray Him. In spite of His mission of liberation, at the end of His three-year campaign, almost everyone on earth had lined up against Him.

It was at that point that Jesus mounted the ultimate battle when He climbed a hill called Calvary. At first, the enemy thought that getting Jesus to Calvary Hill would prove to be the key to victory. In fact, to most casual observers, it appeared as if Jesus had lost the battle there. Soldiers of the enemy captured Him and horribly beat Him. They even pressed thorns into His head that mockingly represented a crown. They spit on Him, cursed Him, and eventually, right at the top of Calvary Hill, nailed His hands and feet to a rugged, wooden cross, where He died.

Later that day, Jesus' lifeless body was laid in a borrowed tomb. As the tomb was sealed, the enemy began to celebrate. At the same time, the squad that had joined up with Jesus became scared, disillusioned, and unsure of what to do next. It appeared as if the enemy had won and that its tyrannical hold on the world would be complete and secure. Maybe

Jesus wasn't the greatest soldier who ever lived after all!

But three days later there was a rumble. At first it was barely audible. Then it began to crescendo. He's alive! He's alive! He's alive! Jesus was alive again! He had defeated the grave, and death, and sin—something that only God could do. Frank explained to me that just as we fought to defeat Fascism, Jesus died and rose again to defeat sin.

No, sin is not completely gone. There are still battles going on, because some of the enemy's soldiers have not yet accepted the fact that the war is over. But Jesus did indeed win it all when He made the ultimate sacrifice on Calvary Hill.

On account of Jesus' sacrifice, He opened the most amazing door of opportunity imaginable. He enabled people to be freed from sin's bondage and experience an eternal relationship with God. Anyone can take advantage of this opportunity by simply believing in the Lord Jesus Christ for the forgiveness of sin and the gift of eternal life.

I've now come to realize that the opportunity to receive eternal life makes all of the opportunities that we have experienced in America since World War II seem very insignificant.

As I listened to Frank tell me the story of Jesus, my first reaction was to argue. Being a lawyer, I began my defense. I told Frank that when I thought about God, I didn't think that I needed Him to rescue me. I had done a pretty good job of supplying your grandmother and me with a very comfortable lifestyle. I was successful and well respected within the community. Why did I need God? I wasn't that bad!

Much to my surprise, Frank disposed of my argument without much effort. He explained that while I had done a good job of meeting my own earthly *wants*, my earning power was incapable of meeting my one real *need*, which was to overcome the sin that was a part of my very nature. Only God could handle that task, which is why He sent His only Son, Jesus. When God gives, He meets our deepest need.

Tom, that morning in the United States cemetery at Normandy, France, I lost an argument with Frank and won the war of life. I bowed next to a white cross that marks the grave of an American soldier and asked God to forgive me of my sin and grant to me the gift of eternal life. It was an amazing and incredibly emotional experience. I received the opportunity for which Jesus had sacrificed it all.

Your grandmother had made a similar

choice about following Jesus several years earlier. In fact, as I would learn later, she was the one who had asked Frank to explain Jesus' story to me that morning. While I thought she was asleep in our hotel room, she was actually on her knees the whole time, praying that I would trust Jesus as my Savior!

Tom, I don't know why, but I have almost as hard a time talking about my faith in Christ as I do talking about the battles I was in during World War II. But you're my only grandson, and the one who will probably inherit a lot of the physical and financial opportunities that I have worked hard to build. Most of all, I want to pass on to you the heritage of faith.

While the opportunities of a free and prosperous country and a profitable law practice may last a lifetime, the opportunity for a relationship with God will last for eternity. Please, Tom, discover this truth: that love leads to sacrifice, and sacrifice leads to opportunity.

When Frank and I got back to the hotel, he showed me a verse in the Bible that I had heard before but never thought much about. It's John 3:16. It says, *"For God so loved the world, that he gave his only begotten Son, that whosoever believeth in him should not perish but have everlasting life."* At long last, I fully realized that it was God Who started this amazing progression of love and sacrifice that created for me such a wonderful opportunity.

My only regret is that I didn't come to accept the truth about Jesus much earlier in my life. I've had so little time to make up for my years of unbelief. Your grandmother died less than a year after our life-changing trip to France. How I wish we could have lived our entire married life with a mutual commitment to the love and sacrifice of God!

In spite of my regrets, I am looking toward the future with great hope. Not that my cancer will be cured. I've come to terms with the fact that I am going to die pretty soon. What I'm looking forward to is going to Heaven. I'm starting to feel a little bit like I did on the train heading home in 1945.

I'm going Home. I'm going to see your

grandmother again. And I'm going to have a face-to-face meeting with the greatest soldier who ever lived!

Tom, my life has been changed and shaped by two wars—one in Europe, the other at Calvary. My prayer today is that you too will experience the opportunity that God's love and sacrifice have made possible.

Please don't fall for the idea that God is the kind of judge who weighs the evidence to see if you've been good or bad. Heaven is not reserved for those who act good, but for those who are forgiven. No degree of goodness can earn eternal life. It's all about faith, which means trusting solely in Jesus' sacrifice on the cross instead of trusting in your own moral or generous behavior.

Jesus said, *"I am the way, the truth, and the life; no man cometh unto the Father, but by Me."* Jesus also said, *"I am the Door."* Jesus is the only way. I remember Frank telling me that the Door is open to everyone, but there is only one Door, and His name is Jesus Christ. Only Jesus is the Son of God; only

Jesus died on the cross to pay the penalty for sin; and only Jesus rose from the grave.

Please don't make the same mistakes that I made. Don't pretend that you don't need God. Don't be a father who is hardly ever at home. Don't convince yourself that working long hours for financial reward or the applause of men is worth it. If you will trust in Christ, He will change your life. Your heart will be filled with more love for Carla and the kids than you could have ever imagined. You'll also desire to sacrifice to meet their needs, not as an obligation, but as a demonstration of God's love flowing through you to them.

Tom, while my generation may have sacrificed to make it possible for you to grow up in the greatest country on earth, Jesus' sacrifice makes it possible for you to grow up in the greatest kingdom in eternity. That's the legacy that I want you to learn from me, and pass on for generations to come. Please trust in the Jesus with Whom I am now living!

Love, *Grandpa*

❖   ❖   ❖

AFTER READING my grandfather's letter, I sat on the chair in my bedroom with tears streaming down my cheeks. His words led to so many questions. There were now so many things that I wanted to be able to say to him. In hindsight, his many invitations to visit were obviously attempts to share his story with me. Why had I always claimed to be so busy?

One thing my grandfather hadn't known was the depth of my searching. On the outside, my life looks pretty good. I am a successful attorney, and I am enjoying the material opportunities that my grandfather's generation planted. What I *don't* need is my grandfather telling me that I am a sinner who needs help.

In spite of the external appearance though, my life is a mess. My relationship—if you can call it that—with my wife is cold and distant. I have three incredibly beautiful and bright kids, but I barely know them.

Sadly, just before I got the call that my

grandfather had died, my wife learned of my involvement with another woman. The revelation was devastating. She was angry, told me that our marriage was over, and asked me to leave.

Then we received word of my grandfather's death. Our need to go to the funeral put our plans to separate on hold for the time being. Carla put on a good front at the funeral, but her mind was made up. I couldn't blame her for feeling the way she did; after all, our marriage had been emotionally dead for a long time.

The irony of it all was that I probably wouldn't have found the photograph of my grandfather had it not been for the need to pack my things to leave. It was in the suitcase that I had taken to the funeral!

As I sat there reading my grandfather's last words, my life was in shambles, my marriage was over, and my future looked bleak. I was an attorney trained to argue, but it didn't take much to convince me that I needed what my grandfather's letter described. I began to wish that I had a friend like Frank.

After reading the letter, I didn't know what to do, so I decided to go outside for a long walk. I wanted to believe in what my grandfather had explained, but my life seemed to be too far gone for forgiveness. Why would God want to spend His love on a mess like me? I had tried to change before. I'd tried lots of self-help gimmicks and made a lot of empty promises; but every time, after the hype wore off, I'd fall back into the same old self-destructive habits again. Why should

I think that trying God would be any different?

When I got back to the house, I decided to do something that seemed ridiculous, but I had nothing to lose. I tracked down Frank's phone number. He was still alive and living in a retirement community just outside Phoenix. Then I did something even more ridiculous. I went to visit him.

I am writing this while on a plane headed home from Phoenix. I spent all day yesterday with Frank. My grandfather was right; he's quite a guy. He told me the whole story about my grandpa and him during the war, and then he told me about the greatest soldier who ever lived.

Last night, Jesus rescued me from my prison camp of sin. Today I'm both excited and scared. I'm excited because I have an eternal home to go to someday. But I'm also scared because I'm not sure that I'll be able to repair the damage that my selfishness has caused in my home on earth.

Just before boarding the plane, I talked

with my wife on the phone. I told her about my grandfather's letter, my visit with Frank, and my new faith in Jesus.

Through a river of tears I asked Carla to forgive me and I tried to express my new desire for God's love and sacrifice to flow through me to her and our kids. Although she is not ready to forget the past, she is willing to give the future one more chance.

The plane is getting ready to land, and I feel a little bit like my grandfather must have felt when he rode that train home after World

War II. Finally, for me, the war is over, and thanks to the greatest soldier who ever lived, I'm going home.

HOW TO BECOME
A CHRISTIAN

THE BIBLE DESCRIBES three key steps in becoming a Christian.

I MUST:

Admit that I am a sinner, unable to live up to God's standard of perfection and, therefore, deserving of eternal separation from God.

"For all have sinned, and come short of the glory of the God" (Romans 3:23).

"For the wages of sin is death; but the gift of God is eternal life through Jesus Christ our Lord" (Romans 6:23).

 Acknowledge that Jesus is God's only Son who died on the cross to pay the penalty for my sin. He arose from the grave three days later in victory over death.

"But God commendeth his love toward us in that, while we were yet sinners, Christ died for us" (Romans 5:8).

"Christ died for our sins according to the scriptures; and that he was was buried, and that he rose again the third day, according to the scriptures" *(1 Corinthians 15:3, 4).*

 Believe in Jesus Christ alone for the forgiveness of my sins and the gift of eternal life in heaven.

"For God so loved the world, that he gave his only begotten Son, that whosoever believeth in him should not perish, but have everlasting life" *(John 3:16).*

"For whosoever shall call upon the name of the Lord shall be saved" (Romans 10:13).

❖   ❖   ❖

IF YOU ARE READY to become a Christian, honestly believing each of the statements above to be true, then pray from your heart the following prayer:

"God in Heaven, I know that I am a sinner, and I understand that my sin deserves to be severely punished. But because of your love, Jesus took my punishment when He died on the cross. Please forgive me of my sin and give me the gift of

eternal life. Thank you for hearing my prayer and receiving me into your family. Amen."

WELCOME to God's family! Please quickly contact a trusted Christian friend or church, and tell them about your belief in Christ.

P.O. Box 882 • Kokomo, IN 46903-0882

ABOUT THE AUTHOR
DANIEL JOHNSON has pastored local churches in Illinois and Indiana. He currently ministers in Kokomo, Indiana, where he resides with his wife, Linda, and their four children.

ORDERING INFORMATION

To order additional copies of
The Greatest Soldier Who Ever Lived,

CALL TOLL-FREE

1-877-408-7038

WEB SITE:

www.providencepubl.com

MAILING ADDRESS:

P.O. Box 882

Kokomo, IN 46903-0882